A Guide to Happy Family Camping

A Guide to Happy Family Camping

A little help to get started
camping with kids

TAMMERIE SPIRES

Good Books

Intercourse, PA 17534

Design by Dawn J. Ranck
Cover illustration by Cheryl Benner

A GUIDE TO HAPPY FAMILY CAMPING
Copyright © 1998 by Good Books, Intercourse, PA 17534
International Standard Book Number: 1-56148-248-X
Library of Congress Catalog Card Number: 98-11431

Library of Congress Cataloging-in-Publication Data

Spires, Tammerie.
    A guide to happy family camping : a little help to get started camping with
kids / Tammerie Spires.
        p. cm.
    ISBN 1-56148-248-X
    1. Camping.   2. Family recreation.   I. Title.
GV191.7.S65   1998
796.54--dc21   98-11431
                                                                          CIP

Dedication

To my David, Harper, and Chandler,
who put the family in family camping for me

Acknowledgments

About a year ago I decided to leave a corporate career I loved for two other jobs I love even more: Mom and Writer. This would never have been my idea, but has proved to be an enormous blessing, so I am thankful to God for drawing me to this path.

I am deeply grateful to have grown up on a farm where I learned a love of the out-of-doors; thanks, Mom and Dad. I thank Camp Lula Sams and Camp Mystic for my early camping experiences, and my husband, David, for getting us into camping as a family.

I appreciate, too, the other families we have camped or shared ideas with: Steve and Judy Baldauf, Kim Lin and Jerry Sovich, Susan and Dan Sellers, Pat and Gary Coleman, Shannon and Rebecca Spires, Clay and Crystal Spires, and much-loved neighbors Yvonne and Clark Roberts, and Wayne and Annette Albrecht.

I am also glad to have had a cheering section vicariously hiking along this journey from Career Mom to Writer Mom with me. Their companionship and encouragement have meant a great deal: Mary Burkhead, Janee Duval, Kimberly Fairchild, Adriana Mutolo Hartley, Beth Miles, Julie Richmond, Elizabeth Bryant Robinson, and Elayne Vick.

And what a wonder it's been to work with the folks at Good Books. Merle and Phyllis Good and designer Dawn Ranck have exhibited a great deal of enthusiasm for this project and more than a little patience with me!

Lastly, to three people who have inspired and shared my love of writing: Mrs. Sammy Roiz, my sixth-grade English teacher, who tried to give me an understanding of the tools of language and writing; John Trimble, my writing professor at the University of Texas at Austin, who taught me a great respect for the reader; and finally Roger Lipsey, a wise mentor, caring compadre, and friend of the heart who has been generous in sharing his wisdom and support for many years.

— Tammerie Spires

Table of Contents

Camping with Kids . . . WHY?   3

Six Happy Camper Principles   7

1. Planning   9

2. Roadtrip   19

3. Food   27

4. Play   37

5. Gear   51

6. Sleep   65

7. Conclusion   69

8. Resources: Additional Information You Might
   Find Useful

   — The Lists: Planning, Packing,   71
     and Preparing

   — Magazines, Catalogs, and Web Sites   77

   — Alphabetical List of U.S. Parks   85
     and Wildlife Departments and Canadian
     National Parks

About the Author   106

Camping With Kids . . . WHY?

Maybe you've never camped before but think it might be something fun to do with the kids. Maybe you used to camp with your spouse, but you're just not sure it's going to work out with an infant or toddler. Maybe you've camped quite a bit with your kids, and you're curious to know if there are better ways to handle the tricky moments.

This book's for you. In it you'll discover bright ideas and basic necessities that will help novice and pro alike have more fun and less fuss outdoors. We'll cover six Happy Camper Principles, 90 handy tips, information about places to go, some stories about where we've been, and a few lists of stuff and things to remember, get, do, or see (in the real world and on the Internet). Check Section 8, Resources, for these.

What you won't find is any preconception about the "right" way to camp. If Madison Avenue has its way with you, you may think you have to be a senior citizen in an air-conditioned rolling palace or a Gen-Xer, hanging your ultra-light, four-season tent off the side of a glacier.

The fact is, you don't have to go to either of those extremes to get out of your house and out of your norm and have a great time doing it, especially if you have the nerve to take your kids and a little infrastructure with you.

What kind of infrastructure? Well, that depends on you. Which leads us to **Happy Camper Principle I:** *Camping happily requires determining what you need to camp happily.* Back seat of a car? Tent? Truck bed? Van seat? Pop-up trailer? Hard-side trailer? Big-league RV or motor home? There's a continuum here, ranging from sleeping under the stars to sleeping under the TV aerial. You decide where you need to be. And if you hear somebody snickering over how little or how much you have . . . laugh back at 'em in the secure knowledge that you have what you need to be happy.

There are lots of us in the generations between the Rolling Retired and Gen-X who sort of camped when we were kids, and who really want to sort of camp with *our* kids. Jim Shahin called it "Camping in Quotes" in an *American Way* magazine column.

Happy Camper Principle I:

Camping happily requires determining what you need to camp happily.

My husband and I both "camped" as kids: Dave in his grandmother's back pasture with other neighborhood hoodlums, during the formative years when Dinty Moore and Dr. Pepper satisfied all major food group requirements; Tam in various Girl Scout and non-Scout girl camps, with roles ranging from bookish Brownie-sized bug-tracker to quasi-adult waterfront counselor.

We started camping again soon after our daughter was born (Harper, 1993), though we didn't take her with us at first. Our first serious Camping Trip was intended to give a couple of new parents a break from the beloved four-month-old. But with a few successes under our respective belts, we soon wanted to share the fun with Harper and the new rug-rat, Chandler (1995). That's when we started learning the lessons you'll find in this book, about everything from planning to food to fun to gear.

I hope this book kindles your desire to camp with kids. If you're ready to hit the road and pitch camp, then read on, head out, and let us hear *your* adventures!

Six
Happy Camper
Principles

1. Camping happily requires determining what you need to camp happily.

2. Make and use lists.

3. Everything should be fun . . . make it so.

4. The more situations you are prepared for, the more you are prepared to enjoy.

5. Everybody over two years of age packs her own stuff.

6. Sleep is an important prerequisite to having fun on a camping trip. Make sure the kids and the adults get plenty.

1.

Planning

Most parents know that living with kids is the Great Multiplier. You're twice as late . . . or you've learned to start getting ready twice as early. Well, add camping to the mix, and you've got the Mucho Multiplier. You need four times as much underwear, but you're having four times as much fun. How can you make the Mucho Multiplier work for you? Here you go . . .

1. The key to happy camping with kids can be found in the three Ps: Planning, Packing, and Preparing. Think through where you want to go, what you'll do when you get there, and what you'll need to have with you to enjoy the experience.

    Write it down as you go, because the secret of successful planning, packing, and preparing is . . . *The List.* This one is important enough to be **Happy Camper Principle II:** *Make and use lists.* Lists save lives, hair, and marriages!

Happy Camper Principle II:

Make and use lists.

2. I put my master list together in three columns, headed: Week Before, Day Before, and Day Of. I fold it to the appropriate time frame, and it all gets done.

    Put an underline, dash, or hollow bullet next to items on your list, and check them off as they are packed or performed. Don't just cross things off by drawing a line through them. You'll forget what those items were and peer at them to see what it was you've already done.

3. Be sure everybody is clear on who's doing what. Mark it on the list if you need to. My list also includes some blank lines at the end so I can customize my reminders for each specific trip.

    Do take your list on the road with you, so you don't forget what you forgot. (When diapers are what you forgot, once is enough!)

4. While a computer is a very expensive list-making device (in the way that a microwave is a very expensive popcorn popper), an easily revisable list is an eminently useful list. My list is on the computer, but I'd write it by hand if necessary. It's that important. (See Resources, pages 71-75 for sample lists; chances are I've already missed much of what you need!)

5. Equally important is what not to take. Don't take crap. No brain drains (TV, video games, and pretty much everything else requiring batteries, except

Pine Whispers

Shortly after Harper was born, Dave and I took a much needed trip together sans baby (thanks, Grandmother Nan!). It was a harbinger of things to come. We hightailed it to Arkansas' Petit Jean State Park, a mountaintop camp nestled lakeside among a forest of pine trees.

I found it a great joy and relief to be set loose in the outdoors, after a few months spent mostly around the house being an over-protective, anxious first-time mom with a new baby. Dave and I happily stomped pine-shaded hiking trails and swept pine needles out of our food.

On Sunday morning before the long drive back to Texas, we sat with other campers on a row of benches in a piney grove for an early worship service. I don't remember much of what the preacher said, but I do remember the pines whispering, as they'd whispered all weekend long. "Come back," they said. "Bring the child. Come back outside where you belong." I was reminded that Spirit uses whatever means necessary to call us to where we need to be.

Harper and I started getting outside more often, and I wasn't so afraid of being a mom out in the wide, wide world.

your flashlights and weather radio). No junk food for the body (tell the kids it's their first spa weekend). No attitudes. This is the tough one. Babies don't like schedules to get out of whack . . . toddlers are bored by the drive . . . kids miss the TV . . . 'tweens think the great outdoors is geeky . . . teens believe a weekend with their parents is time off in hell. You name it, they'll whine about it. Unless they are busy.

Everybody gets a little responsibility, everybody pitches in to get the chores done, and everybody has a whole lot of fun. Keep it easygoing, and a little latitude will help the attitude.

6. Dave and I have found that the buddy system works well; we're a good team. If you're a single parent, think about doubling up. There's not much a couple of moms or a pair of dads flying in tandem can't manage. You can certainly manage everything in this book.

Even pairs of parents may want to partner up. We have several friends we like to camp with . . . because we like them, because we're compatible campers, and because they love us and our kids enough to baby-sit during the occasional nap while Dave and I get a rare chance to mountain-bike or swim together . . . *alone!*

7. Scheduling is a big part of camp planning. This makes some of our childless friends and relatives

crazy, since they want to go and do at any hour of the day. Well, we used to do that, but we've learned it's not really fair to the kids, and it can pretty much ruin your day. (Just try setting out on a three-mile hike at nap-time.)

Nowadays, serendipity is what happens when well rested families with sufficient snacks, diapers, and dry changes of clothes meet a stream crossing to an alternative trail. Serendipity, yes, but with planning and room for error.

8. Speaking of scheduling, if you've developed a Fear of Five O'Clock, hang on to it. You need a healthy respect for the time between 5:00 p.m. and bedtime. This is *not* the time to schedule a hike, swim, or even a side trip in the car.

Don't try to do anything but **have fun doing what *must* be done:** make dinner, feed kids, clean up kids, rig for nighttime, put kids to bed. The fact is, if you can get through the Fearful Five O'Clock hour intact, you've got it made.

9. Routine helps, but be flexible. Our system of putting both kids to bed together at the same time had to be adjusted when the youngest, Chandler, got to the gonzo giggle stage (11 months old). He and his older sister, Harper, kept each other up for hours, rocking the trailer with their laughter. We finally had to keep her up long enough for him to fall asleep first, at which time we snuck her into

The January Thaw

In the January of Chandler's first year, the weatherman forecast a weekend we couldn't resist. Even as far south as we live, January's weather is commonly raw, bitterly cold. So when we heard "highs in the 70s on Saturday," we begged and borrowed a pop-up from our neighbors Wayne and Annette and headed to nearby Mineral Wells State Park. Wayne and Annette joined us for the day, and we took turns watching the kids and mountain-biking. Then adults and children headed out for a late afternoon hike around Lake Mineral Wells, through winter-denuded trees.

At sunset, we were glad the leaves lay a-tangle on the ground, because sun and sky were putting on a show. As the sun fell toward the hills on the other side of the lake, streamers of clouds high and low turned burnished gold against a blush pink sky. The lake, rippled by the wind into wavelets, reflected a scattering of pink and gold, the pattern shifting like a tumbling blocks quilt. We stood on the hiking trail for an hour, grown-ups and children enraptured into a still wonder.

January melted our hearts that day.

her bunk. Now that Harper is four and Chandler is two, the only technique that works is to wear 'em both out before bedtime so they're too tired to giggle for long.

10. Packing is another big part of camp planning. After all, The List is primarily to help you remember what to pack, and then to actually pack it, preferably where you can remember to find it.

A little practice and forethought will help you pack efficiently enough to justify bringing everything you know you'll need, and most of what you think you might want. Think flexible and reusable. Handy Tip #74 below explains our multiple uses for big Rubbermaid tubs, for example.

11. *Stay packed* and you'll go more often. We keep our trailer loaded with what we call *permanent stocks:* camp bedding, hiking boots, child carrier, camp chairs, towels . . . and *replenishable stocks:* non-perishable food staples, RV toilet paper, spare set of toiletries . . . You'll find other ideas in Resources, pages 72 and 73.

We've found that the easier it is to go, the more often we go, and the more often we go, the happier we are. And the happier we are . . . well, that is the point, isn't it?

12. Work with your kids to plan and pack their backpacks: for car trips and for each hike. Help the kids

load their packs for the car trip, so each has his or her own books, blocks, and other anti-road-boredom devices.

Then, prior to the first hike, reload with hiking requirements, like water, snacks, dipes and wipes, Band-Aids . . . whatever the kid needs, within reason.

13. *Pack foods you know your family likes to eat,* and which you'll be equipped to cook and clean up after easily. Some kids like hot dogs. Ours don't. Your kids may love roasted marshmallows. Well, one of mine likes 'em raw as a foam pillow, and the other won't go near 'em (yeah, the same kid who won't eat cake icing). But they both *love* pasta with pesto, they'll pick a chicken clean, and they'll snarf S'mores ingredients a la carte.

We'll talk more about food in the next section, but the key point here is: *Pack foods you know your family likes to eat.*

14. Finally, a side benefit to family camping is how much more you will appreciate camping *without* kids. Yes, occasionally you should invest in a baby-sitter for a long four-day weekend and take your mate out for a spin.

What does this have to do with planning? Well, if you're doing the planning, sneak in a few nice surprises—a fly-fishing guide for a day, steaks instead of burgers, a luxury shampoo to wash her

Campfire Stories

One cold winter night, after putting the tired small fry to bed, Dave and I sat around a piñon bonfire with brother Shannon and sis-in-law Rebecca. We were wreathed in resinous smoke, delighting in the smells and noises of the night.

A campfire usually inspires the Spires brothers to tell tales of their childhoods and teenage lunacies. However, Dave had recently discovered the master storyteller, J. Frank Dobie. We found that Dobie's *Apache Gold and Yaqui Silver* is especially effective by firelight. Passing the book around the circle, we took turns reading out loud far into the night.

By the way, if you come upon suspected bank robbers in the deep of night out West, don't bother searching their saddlebags for the gold. It's probably buried in the last place you'd look: under their campfire. Just ask Mr. Dobie!

hair a la Redford in *Out of Africa,* Ghirardelli truffles instead of S'mores—whatever *your* beloved would prize.

2.
Roadtrip

Unless you are camping in your backyard (in which case, all other sections apply *except* this one!), you are facing a drive to your camp site. We have traveled anywhere from hours to a day to get to a camping spot and find that you need to make pretty much the same preparation for a two-hour trip as a 10-hour trip. Just be ready to cycle through your entertainment ideas a few more times, and a little extra patience and understanding doesn't hurt.

The roadtrip is your whole trip in microcosm. It can involve eating, sleeping, all the interesting body functions, little side trips, micro-hikes in parks or small town squares along the way, and it should definitely involve fun. I know parents who drug their kids with Benadryl or videos to get through a long roadtrip, but, really, that's not necessary. Try a few of these ideas, and see if they help.

15. *Get off to a good start.* A journey well begun is halfway done, someone once said, and I agree. The whole day seems to go better when we get off to a rollicking good start, but that doesn't happen by accident. Use your lists to get as much done and packed as you can in the days before the Final

Launch Countdown.

As you're finishing loading on the morning of departure, go ahead and buckle the kids in the car. This will get them out of the way, and trigger last minute issues like, "Mom, I forgot my baby-doll!," and "Dad, I have to go to the bathroom!," before the actual last minute.

16. *Getting off early helps.* When we're trying to get an obscenely early start, Dave and I get up and load while the munchkins sleep, then throw them into clean clothes (laid out the night before, natch) and strap 'em into their seats. While Dave does the final 10 minutes, I feed the kids a snack breakfast (milk, bananas, granola or Nutri-grain bars, Pop-Tarts, toast, toaster waffles, whatever), and we hit the road.

    The kids find this sort of rapid launch sequence fascinating, especially with our family yell as we head out the driveway: "Rock and roll!"

17. If you have trouble getting up early, console yourself with the thought that the time you've saved leaving at 7:00 a.m. instead of 9:00 a.m. can be spent having fun along the way, which leads me to my next point.

18. *Slow down.* The fact is, especially with small kids, you are going to have to stop and let them out to stretch, change diapers, and all that other stuff. So

Traveling in Time

We like camping in cold weather, but don't usually travel out into snowstorms on purpose. However, on one trip to the West we managed to catch a late spring snowstorm outside Albuquerque.

Coming down out of the mountains, we were sure the snow would stop or turn to rain. However, as we entered I-40, we saw a gloppy mess of an interstate, marked only by a parallel track of ruts leading east. We fell into them, proceeded around a bend in the canyon and saw . . . a parking lot. Stretching for miles ahead of us, all we saw were the taillights of stopped cars, trucks, semis, and RVs.

It didn't get better anytime soon. We took three hours to travel the next 20 miles. But after awhile, it wasn't the miles that mattered. It was the hours. As motionless reality set in, people began to climb out of their vehicles. We commiserated, hurled snowballs, sculpted snow folks, and patiently cooperated our way out of the storm.

So much for road rage. The traffic may have snarled, but the people didn't. I was proud of us all, as we proved that it's not the problem that is important, it's the perspective.

you may as well build the time for it into the schedule of whoever in your family is anal about time. Plan fun things to do when you stop, and time spent in the car will be easier.

We recently did a Springfield-to-Dallas (that includes Illinois, Missouri, Oklahoma, and Texas for those of you filling out a sticker map) run in 14 hours. Never mind that my in-laws do it in 12. I think the longer trip was actually easier on our little ones because it involved some serious rest/eat/play stops along the way.

19. If you get off at a roadside stop, bring out some chalk for hopscotch or sidewalk art. Let the kids take pictures or draw pictures. Examine weird bugs together. Read the historical markers. Play tire bingo (ask any tour bus driver how if you've forgotten). Crank up the car radio and do aerobics or the Hokey-Pokey. (See Chapter 4, "Play," page 37, for more ideas.)

     Trout Fishing in America has great kids' music that parents can stand to listen to. See who learns to count the *18 Wheels on the Big Rig* first—you or the kids!

20. *Get off the interstate* and take the back roads. Whenever we have time (and we do try to build time into our travel plans), we make getting there a big part of the fun by taking the *Blue Highways* approach.

You may remember this book by William Least Heat-Moon. He took a few months to drive a big loop around the US, taking only "blue highways" wherever he could: "On the old highway maps of America, the main routes were red and the back roads blue. Now even the colors are changing. But in those brevities just before dawn and a little after dusk—times neither day nor night—the old roads return to the sky some of its color. Then, in truth, they carry a mysterious cast of blue, and it's that time when the pull of the blue highway is strongest, when the open road is a beckoning, a strangeness, a place where a man can lose himself."

21. Women and kids like getting lost, too. Sometimes it's the roads we didn't mean to take that get us where we want to go. Try it. Once you slow down, the little towns you pass through will intrigue rather than irritate you. Try the pie at the Round Top Cafe while your kids cavort around the old roadhouse in the square at Round Top, Texas.

22. *Pack books.* We set a big box of books between the two car seats in the back, and this keeps the kids occupied until we can get out of Dallas traffic (always my husband's least favorite part of the trip). Then, periodically through the day, one or both will pick up books and entertain themselves. We especially like when Harper gets one of the

Carl books by Alexandra Day and tells us stories from what she sees. And Chandler still likes to read Dr. Seuss upside down, as if the good doctor's books weren't odd enough. We're probably going to have to get counseling for the kid someday, but for now, this works.

23. *Pack a few toys.* Pick these car toys carefully for maximum play value and ease of cleanup. A great choice for toddlers and up are the Lauri products (Call 800/451-0520 for a free catalog). Lauri makes crepe rubber learning puzzles and lacing toys. The kids have fun with them, and they are oh-so-quiet and easy to clean and put away.

    My friend Pat always kept the best car toys and a few books hidden away altogether between car trips for fresh fun.

24. *Pack car snacks,* and be prepared to vacuum. I keep trying to: (a) find snacks the kids like that make less of a mess, and (b) help Dave have a sense of humor about what he finds between and under the seats ("Honey, think of it as an archaeological dig. You're seeing the history of our trips!" "Grrr.") I fail on both counts. But the trips are happy. We do pretzel sticks, raisins, Goldfish, apples, grapes, bars, whatever works.

25. *Naps are good.* It's hard for the kids to nap in their car seats, but we keep 'em in there for safety's

Wait Five Minutes . . . It'll Change

The weather, that is.

On one of our trips, the sky poured all the first day, causing some of our party to bolt for home. We were rewarded for sticking it out with three crisp fall days of rain-washed clarity. Another trip we spied an approaching front just in time to scurry camper-wards before the storm hit with a brief but intense fury. This storm's passage left a luminescent greenish glow over land and sky and dropped the temperature 20 degrees.

But the highlight of our weather wonders has to be Dave's high energy experience. We had just set up camp in a thicket of pines, hurrying to level the trailer before threatening clouds released their deluge. Inside the camper with the kids, I saw a flash of pink concurrent with a loud CRACK of thunder. A moment later, Dave hurried into the camper, looking pale and startled. "Okay, that was close enough," he said, and went on to describe how he'd looked up for no real reason, just in time to see the pine above him struck a-sizzle with lightning. His inexplicable escape was the talk of the camp that weekend.

Close enough, indeed.

sake. Pillows and loveys from home help. Feed 'em a big lunch, and fill the vehicle with gas so you don't have to wake them by stopping. Turn down the music, and let the road sing them to sleep.

26. Every roadtrip ends with camp setup. We finally learned to pay attention to this seemingly insignificant part of the trip on our third outing. It's tricky when your children are small; big ones just help with the setup. The adults will want to work together to set up camp, and the kids will want to run wild. Not a good combination.

Install toddlers and small kids at the site's picnic table with snack and drink while you pitch the tent or level the trailer (yes, you'll need to minimize snacking on the road during the last hour or so). If you have the kind of baby swing with a spring that hangs from a doorway, you'll be glad to know it will also hang from a tree. String the kid up and he'll stay out of trouble. Teeny babies can stay in the car seat, or stretch out in the port-a-crib (you packed it last for easy access, remember?).

After setup, take a little walk to stretch the kinks out, even if you've made an evening arrival.

3.
Food

Some of you are going to want to laugh at this section. May I refer you back to the opening pages, "Camping with Kids . . . WHY?", Happy Camper Principle I: *Camping happily requires determining what you need to camp happily.*

Cooking and eating good food is one of my favorite things to do, so I minimize the work involved, but I don't eliminate it. Knowing that, you may want to look in this section for ideas and principles you can apply in your own way.

27. My kids are still at the three-squares- and three-snacks-a-day stage, so it can seem that the trip revolves around food. But by remembering the three P's of camp chow—planning, packing, and preparing—we do manage to have a little fun in between.

    Think through your trip day by day and night by night—what you'll be doing, where you'll be going, what you'll need to take to eat, and what kind of preparation and cleanup that food will require.

28. As mentioned in #13, food you know your family likes is best. Yes, you can try some campier items

than you eat in your at-home diet, but don't strand yourself in the great outdoors with nothing but camp food that only your spouse will eat (out of misguided loyalty!).

If you do want to rely on trail mix and gorp, try it a few times at home to see who's going to be a happy camper and who might need a little mac and cheese to survive.

29. *Breakfast.* We have two kinds of breakfast: break-*fast* (quick: food *prior* to entertainment) and break-fast (slow: food *as* entertainment). Breakfast is one of our favorite meals of the day, but starting off with a big breakfast can eat up half the morning. And morning is Kid Prime Time, when my kids are most rested, happy, and ready for adventure. So we toss down some granola bars and bananas, beverage of choice, and hit the trail.

But when you wake up to a rainy, foggy, or frigid day, sometimes a big breakfast is in order, with better weather by the time you're set to roll out. Big breakfast ideas include standards like pancakes and ham, and personal favorites like breakfast tacos. An added benefit: Most big breakfasts make great leftovers for snacks or lunch, thereby saving time later.

30. We take snacks *whenever* we leave camp. We can always figure on needing them mid-morning (yep, for those of you who are counting, that's *right* after

breakfast), again after nap-time in the afternoon, maybe a little snack as a late dinner comes together, or right before bed if dinner was early.

On walkabout, we take granola bars, pretzels, raisins, and apples. Crackers are good, too, but don't seem to give the kids much going power, and they shatter easily (though small crackers like Goldfish are portable and can cheer up a grumpy kid). Bananas are great snacks in camp, but too smushy for backpacking.

31. We also take water whenever we leave camp. We usually carry a squeeze bottle in every backpack and keep a couple more jugs in the back of the truck (for refilling drinking bottles, and for rinsing sandy feet or dirty hands).

32. Water is one of those things you really can't have enough of, and that includes the frozen variety. A tip: The ice-maker in our fridge at home seems to have been designed for a family of eight, which we usually are not. When it begins to overflow, we load up Zip-loc bags with ice and keep them in our extra freezer out in the garage. These ice bags go straight into the ice chest with anything we want to keep frozen or cold on the roadtrip to the camp site. Then, as the bags thaw, we can always pour clean, ice-cold water out into a cup, or lay an icy bag over a boo-boo.

My friend Pat reuses the stoppered bags her

The Eleventh Commandment

"Thou shalt not live by camp grub alone."

We heed this commandment very seriously when camped within 10 miles of a small town. We'll pick a night to decamp and head into town, looking for the crowded parking lot outside a place with character. No chain, theme, or fast-food restaurants need apply.

One of our best discoveries on the first Caprock Canyons trip was Quitaque's worst-kept secret: the restaurant with no name. During a quick provisioning stop in town, we overheard discussion that the semi-regular Friday night fajita fest was on. Where? Good question. In a tin barn on the main street through town. No name on the wall outside. Just look for a full parking lot on Friday night. And if you run out of guacamole, feel free to wander into the kitchen and get it yourself. The no-name restaurant may be short on help, but it sure is long on good food.

drink mix comes in. She freezes these ahead of time and is able to pour out ice-cold water from the stopper.

33. Lunch is the easiest meal of the day, usually sandwiches and fruit, or leftovers from breakfast or last night's dinner. The trick is to keep it quick, calm, and simple, since with little kids you want to ramp down for a nap, and for bigger kids you want to refuel for a fun afternoon. (The only reason to have a big, complicated lunch is for that to be your afternoon's entertainment, which is rare with kids.)

34. Occasionally we'll do burgers or dogs for lunch, but only if the morning fun was brief and hunger-inducing. Usually we have turkey or ham on good bread, or rolled up in a tortilla around some cheese, with one or more of the following: apples, bananas, raisins, carrots. We usually lunch at our camp site, so this is a good time for a juice box or cup of milk.

   And then it's down for the count! Nap-time, also known as adult-alone-time. Bliss.

35. Dinner can be the toughest meal of the day, because the kids are the most tired and grumpy and the hungriest and least likely to eat. I plan things for dinner that I know they'll want to eat and that will come together quickly, while they have a little snack to ward off the grumpies.

36. Pasta and rice are typical favorites. Our kids love pesto and, of course, mac and cheese, and there are lots of boil-n-serve options for rice. I usually grill some veggies (peppers, tomatoes) and put out raw vegetables (celery and carrot sticks, chopped at home) to snack on. We grill some meat: burgers, weenies, steaks. Sausage is *great* on the grill, and in your eggs the next day.

37. Pre-trip prep is key to quick and simple meat. I buy when the meat's on sale, season or marinate it, and then freeze it in big Zip-loc freezer bags. This can be weeks in advance of a particular trip. I'll plan on grilling it on the second or third night, by which time it has had a chance to thaw.

    You *can* grill chicken; I prefer to bring some baked chicken to avoid dealing with raw chicken in the wild. My baked chicken gives us meat the first night, and lunch for at least Day Two.

38. Resources, beginning on page 71, has a larder list to help you plan and pack what you'd like to prepare, but some ingredients are more important than others. I'll just mention a few of the items we like: a good, all-purpose but flavorful *cheese* (sharp cheddar is good for snacking and plain meal-enhancing), a baked *chicken* (do it yourself or from your store's rotisserie; you'll get two-to-four meals out of it), really good *bread* (make it yourself or find a local craft bakery), and your favorite, really good,

Cheap Kitchen Remodel

I always thought my kitchen was too small. It *is* small. Two people do not fit in it at once without bumping elbows or other appendages. Then I started getting really good at feeding four or more people using a two-burner camp stove, the coals in a fire-ring, and the contents of an ice chest. Plus, I had fun doing it.

It's funny how capacious my kitchen seems now whenever I come home from a camping trip. It's been a good reminder for me: abundance is a state of mind, and intentional simplicity helps keep me there.

strong *coffee.* (Pick your luxury; Starbucks Gold Coast blend is one of ours!)

The point here is that if you like food, bring a few of the things you really like. It can rescue a bad day and put the icing on a great day.

39. Don't forget the tools of the trade: we keep our camper stocked with the kitchen tools and utensils we usually need, to prepare the foods we typically bring. Think through your menu ideas to determine which utensils you'll need and put them on your list.

    Don't forget the tools you need for your luxuries; we like our coffee made in a French press, but we also bring decaf espresso for our little campfire espresso maker. We grill a lot, so we are sure to bring our long-handled tongs. A medium-sized serrated knife works best on good bread and ripe tomatoes.

    And then there are the unlikely kitchen invaluables: baby wipes can save water, a kitchen timer can save biscuits (and monitor a kid's time-out).

40. For all your meals and snacks, think extensible. You don't have to limit yourself to what your kids are having, but if you can leverage kid food into adult food, so much the easier for the cook (and the cleaner-upper).

    Stir some spicy sausage into your helping of the kids' noodles. Put some onions and extra sharp cheddar on your burger. Sprinkle some extra pine nuts and garlic on the pesto and fusilli. Pack some peppers into your hot dog's bun.

And after the kids are in bed, kick back with a fruit and cheese plate: Granny Smith apples, walnuts, Maytag bleu cheese, . . . oh, yeah! Real Life is good.

Primitive Art

My years at Camp Lula Sams in Brownsville, Texas, reached their zenith the year I turned 12, finally old enough to "Primitive Camp." The Primitives (as we were appropriately known) proved definitively that Girl Scouts are not weenies. We dug latrines, built bamboo showers, pitched Army canvas tents and cots, and cooked a slew of fire pit dinners. Steak on a Plank, anyone?

Despite being a smoke magnet, I loved fire-tending: setting the buckets of sand and water near the fire pit, digging out the ashes, building the teepee of wood, slipping tinder into the woodpile's crevices, finally coaxing the fire alight, and then, wistfully, respectfully smothering it out after the last S'more.

Canoeing ran a close second to pyromania. Our camp nestled around a *resaca*, a small body of water just big enough to challenge novice canoers. Upon reaching Primitive status and sufficient canoeing skills, we could venture out on a seven-mile canoe trip through the canals and waterways leading out of our familiar *resaca*.

I can see those Primitive joys were signposts for a road I've never wanted to leave, a wondrous blessing for our grown-ups—parents, counselors, administrators, and funders—to have given us.

4.
Play

The prize (you know, the point of camping) you are keeping your eyes on probably includes something like "Being at play in the fields of the Lord." That is, having fun being outside doing things you don't ordinarily do, seeing things you don't ordinarily see, and thinking things you don't ordinarily think about.

Unfortunately, way too many of us have completely forgotten how to have fun. We get so caught up in how something is *supposed* to be that we lose sight of the thing itself. I speak from experience; as you can tell from this book, I like to plan almost as much as I like to do. So I try to live by **Happy Camper Principle III:** *Everything should be fun . . . make it so.*

That includes the planning, the eating, the getting ready, the doing, the cleaning up, the sleeping, the remembering, the planning, and so on. How can I make chores like planning and cleaning up fun, you

Happy Camper Principle III:

Everything should be fun . . . make it so.

ask? Oh, you know. Remember when you were a kid? You were happiest when you were helping a grown-up do an important thing, and when you and the grown-up felt connected doing it.

Hiking tops a lot of lists of things to do on camping trips, and lots of us do it. So most of us know the basics, both for ourselves and for our kids: wear the right attire, avoid chigger and tick territory, take food and water, pack a first-aid kit and a lightweight blanket or ground-cloth. But, just in case, we'll talk about some ideas for how to do these things better or more easily.

Just remember, fun is contagious. Let loving fun permeate everything you do, and pretty soon it'll infect everyone around you.

By the way, we spent an entire section promoting the idea of Roadtrip as Fun. If you skipped that section, go back! Approach your roadtrips as play opportunities, and they will be. Fun, that is.

41. There are people in the world who believe camping is an end in itself. They are *not* parents. You need a prize, and to keep it in plain sight the whole time. Why *do* you want to camp? Be sure it's compelling enough to help you laugh later about chiggers, sunburns, or even rigging diapers out of coffee filters and hand towels. Think about what the kids like to do or try, or, if they're really small, what you'd like them to do or try.

42. Don't forget to be selfish. What do *you* really like to do that you never seem to find time to do at home? *Bring it,* or whatever you need to do it.

    Everybody in my family knows that when it's nap-time, the parents are taking turns baby-sitting, biking, shutterbugging, reading, showering, or just thinking about God, kids, Camping as Real Life . . .

43. In cool weather, dress in layers, and leave room in the pack to store some of those layers out of the way as the day warms up.

    Dress your kids like you dress yourself, maybe with a slightly heavier jacket or one more layer. But don't bundle 'em within an inch of their lives. They'll feel confined, and you'll be carrying a lot of excess outerwear. Kids don't need fancy hiking boots. But a properly fitting shoe with grippy-tread soles and thick socks will prevent stumbles and blisters. (Kids can pack Band-Aids and a little tube of Neosporin just in case.)

44. Speaking of chiggers, don't hike or play in tall grass, or you will be paying with your flesh for the next few weeks, if not months. I do have a couple of unsubstantiated tips: Dave's grandma used to recommend sprinkling shoes and socks with sulfur to keep the little pests away. And my mom and a pharmacist both told me the only thing you can do about chiggers—besides stay away from them—is to strip down immediately after exposure and

Perils of Urban Camping

Dave's youthful camping typically involved a crew gathering at a cow pasture camp site to sleep out. Campfires and homemade "Sterno" sufficed for light, heat, and cooking.

One weekend, after scarfing a record number of Dinty Moores and Wolf Brand Chilis, the boys' thoughts turned to dessert.

"Hey, how 'bout some apples?" And they were off. Across the pasture, over the fence, into the orchard, and up the trees. Soon exclamations of "Yeooww! That's *sour!*" filled the night air. But a wail of sirens cut laughter short, and the scene froze in a squad car's headlights.

"Okay, boys, what's going on!?!"

A moment later one of the miscreants accompanied the officer to the house. Soon guffaws erupted. It was the boy's grandfather, having a laugh at the nervous grandmother who'd called the police on her own grandson, one of the "hoodlums looting the orchard."

Clearly the moral of this story is, "Tell Grandma yourself when camping in her back pasture, because grandpas can be forgetful."

sluice off whatever portion of your anatomy may have been attacked *with rubbing alcohol.* As always, an ounce of prevention is worth pounds of cure.

45. Wear sun-block (SPF 15 or greater) on all exposed skin, and don't forget unlikely territory, such as under your chin and on the tops of your feet. Fact is, everybody has a story to tell about a weird place that got burned. Play it safe, cover it up, and, no, just a hat is not enough.

46. Kids need refueling on the trail pretty regularly. So pack lots of trail-hardy, high-energy snacks and plenty of water. We try to take a brief water break every 15 minutes and a snack break about once an hour.

    How far can kids hike? As far as they are used to. We've usually managed about a mile per year of age.

47. And it is amazing what a walk can do for other kinds of regularity, too. Since all that walking gets all those systems going, be prepared not only to change diapers and/or soiled underwear and clothes, but also to pack these dirtied items back from the trail.

    We bring along our used Zip-loc or other plastic bags, which may not be very environmentally correct, but which are better than leaving the evidence on the scene (and we have seen such evidence).

We also capture and return to camp any trashy remnants of snacks, drinks, or their packaging. Diaper wipes prove invaluable once again for on-the-trail cleanups.

48. *Do pack a first-aid kit* and a lightweight blanket or ground-cloth. The latter comes in handy for diaper changes, snack breaks, naps on unexpectedly long outings, or to protect someone who's been injured. Use common sense on the safety basics; nothing takes the fun out of a hike like getting hurt or lost.

    Use a trail map. If in doubt about the path, turn back immediately.

49. *Don't separate.* Teach the kids to hug a tree (i.e., stay put) and blow a whistle if they do get separated from the adults in the party. Assure them you will backtrack to find them so they will have the confidence to sit tight.

50. *Tuck a disposable camera in each kid's backpack.* At the very least they'll have something fun to do on the hike besides asking if it's almost over. You'll give a preschooler a legitimate show-and-tell entry. You may spur an older kid to satisfy merit badge or extracurricular requirements. You may even ensure the kid has a funny story to tell when she wins her first Pulitzer.

51. We like camping near places to swim in the summertime. Since our kids are small, we are not too

Forests of Fire

What's so amazing about fall-colored trees? Well, not much if you live in New England. But it's not exactly common where we live. Our one stand of maples is so precious that Texas has dedicated a park to them: Lost Maples State Park near the town of Vanderpool. One autumn found us there, amazed at the maple leaves still shining on the trees, the paths astrewn with fiery foliage.

And we found other wonders among the lost maples. One of the trails led to a small lake glimmering under a limestone ledge, tempting anglers and rock-skippers alike. Once downstream from the fisherkids, fishermen, and fisherwomen, Harper and Chandler spent all the precious gravel gathered along the trail. Plink, plink, plunk, and their pockets were empty. But not our memories. That fiery, tree-ringed lake ripples still in our minds.

adventurous about where we swim. We prefer to swim in places intended for swimming; no dangerous undercurrents, no trash-strewn surfaces underfoot. Wearing water shoes is a commonsense precaution. And we hang onto the kids at all times in water over their knees, since they're not swimming yet.

52. We don't like cluttering up the swimming experience with a lot of toys. The fun here is really getting to know this other environment, how it can buoy your body up, how to be safe in it, how to begin learning to make progress through the water.

   So we minimize the inflatables (no inner tubes or air mattresses giving a false sense of security) and keep the toy count down to a bucket and shovel for playing on the beach.

53. If you are camping far from water in the summertime, you just might be crazy enough to use these ideas: I actually saw a family bring an inflatable kids' pool and set it up outside their camper. Another family got creative with a sprinkler and a fan to rig their own mist system. Hey, if summer is when you can camp, you need all the help you can get!

54. Speaking of toy clutter, we have tried to minimize that altogether. We have a rainy-time bucket in the camper with a few toys that have flexible play

Canoe, Take Me Away!

Last spring we spent a long weekend at McGee Creek in Oklahoma with two other families (including a boy Chandler's age named Taylor). On the afternoon of the second day, after herding kids down the hiking trail all morning, we unleashed the canoes we'd brought along and carried them down to the rocky lakeshore.

Harper and Chandler found the canoe a little tippy for a secure ride and couldn't quite deal with having both parents paddle away at once. So the moms and the kids played on a small gravel spit near the camp while the dads took their turn. When the canoe came back, Taylor's mom, Susan, and I elected to have Mother's Day Out on the water.

Though Susan was a novice paddler, we quickly settled into a rhythm and stroked out into the lake to explore the dam and opposite shoreline. We drifted awhile in the middle of the lake, watching the settling birds, shading our eyes from the setting sun, listening to our children's laughter echoing across the lake. We got quite a reception when we paddled back into camp.

For getting away from it all, and then coming back, canoes beat Calgon any day.

value: puzzles, coloring books and colors, blocks. The great outdoors is full of entertainment, after all.

55. On one trip, Harper and her dad assembled a Bug Zoo. This particular camp site was festooned with strange, iridescent purple beetle bugs. She and Dave put one in a jar with some twigs and grass. A sprinkle of water everyday and this purple beetle was quite happy.

    Then Harper found some fuzzy caterpillars. Did you know fuzzy brown and gray caterpillars the size of your pinkie can cohabit with purple beetles? *Harper knows.*

56. One toy that's a special treat: occasionally renting a boat or other watercraft for a couple of hours. I'll never forget the sight of Chandler at 14 months, standing forthrightly in the bow of a party barge on Lake Texoma, the wind blowing his blond curls back, lake spray in his face, his fat little legs spread wide on the deck, the life jacket barely buckling around his rotund torso, toddler epiphany writ large on his face. (Yep, that's the trip I learned to put "disposable waterproof camera" on the packing list!)

57. And then there are campfires. I don't have to describe what you get out of a fire; you're either a pyromaniac or you're not. So bring seasoned firewood with you, and keep it dry.

58. On trips where all our firewood is green or damp, we've snuck in some store-bought fire-starter logs or fatwood kindling to help the fire get going. Yeah, this is cheating, but it's more fun than no fire, and certainly more effective and safer than sprinkling charcoal lighting fluid or lantern fuel on a fire.

59. An afternoon campfire is perfect for kids to help build and enjoy, besides producing perfect coals for dinner-time roasting and grilling. The flickery glow of firelight on a child's face is, well, pretty rhapsodic. Kids love gathering kindling and stacking up a firewood teepee and watching Mom and Dad light the fire.

60. Harper and I like making twig bundles of herb stems after we harvest basil or rosemary from our herb garden. These give the fire interesting smells and smokes.

61. My mom collects pinecones and dips them in cinnamon-scented wax to make firestarters (she bundles these into baskets for Christmas gifts). We have a lot of fun with these on camping trips and in our fireplace at home. They flame up like little Christmas trees. Plain pinecones found at the camp site are entertaining, too.

62. After the kids go to bed, we usually rekindle for an evening fire. Dave and I love campfires under the

Mystic Experiences

Some girls are legacy members of their mothers' sororities. I was a legacy Tonkawa. Let me explain.

I don't actually know if Mom was a Tonk. As the waterfront counselor at Camp Mystic she probably had to maintain an uneasy neutrality. I followed tradition to Mystic as a camper and, therefore, had to choose a tribe. Out of a black bowler I pulled a red slip of paper, and a Tonkawa I was.

This was heartbreaking. The one friend I had made (a day into the six-week term) was a Kiowa. A friendly foe, but An Enemy, nonetheless. Fortunately we managed to remain good friends across enemy lines.

One night near session's end, the Kiowas vanished. They went surreptitiously, until suddenly they were all gone. Then, in the distance, girls' voices. Singing friendship songs, the Kiowas strode in solemn procession back into camp, two by two. The well ordered column broke and scattered, as each Kiowa sought out a sister Tonk and led her to the last campfire of the session. My friend found me.

Candles . . . singing . . . processions . . . bonfires . . . and tears for the end of six weeks we'd remember . . . well, forever. What a night.

stars. Letting your eyes rise from firelight up to starlight will really get you thinking: "Let's see, if we cashed in the 401Ks and the mutual funds, pulled Harper out of preschool, just how long *could* we stay in Real Life ...?"

Giving Thanks

A few years ago, with time off from work in short supply, Dave and I made the risky decision to go camping over Thanksgiving. The long, four day holiday weekend beckoned, and we succumbed to the temptation.

You might be thinking, "Boy, I'd love to do that. But my [insert name here] would just kill me!" Don't be too sure.

Our first camping Thanksgiving drew Dave's brother and sister-in-law, Shannon and Rebecca, out from Albuquerque in their camper to meet us. They brought smoked turkey and fixings since I had my hands full with small kids.

Our second camping Thanksgiving drew my mom, dad, brother Curt, and his family to the town nearest our camp site, where we rendezvous'd with two sets of uncles and aunts for Thanksgiving dinner.

This year? Well, let's just say there are 21 people expected around the Thanksgiving dinner table on Thursday, with about half that number returning to their campers or tents at nearby Kerrville-Schreiner State Park, with the rest staying in nearby hotel rooms. We can hike; they can watch football. Everybody's happy.

So don't be afraid that your family will disown you for abandoning the traditional Thanksgiving. The truth is, they may want to join you!

5.
Gear

Sometimes thinking about gear makes me wonder if I own my stuff, or if my stuff owns me. But then I remind myself about my Happy Camping Principles and try to make sure we all have what we need to be happy.

My own experiences have run the gamut of gear. As a teenager, my Scout troop established a primitive camp. This was Zero Gear. Along the way, Dave and I have camped in tents, cabins, pop-up trailers, even a whale of an RV once. We've settled on a nice little hard-sided trailer, 16 feet of heaven, as far as we're concerned. Moderate Gear.

I am sure that some day Dave and I are going to backpack up into a mountain range, needing only what we can carry. Minimalist Gear. But for now, with our two little ones, our trailer offers the infrastructure that lets us camp really happily. Nobody in our family groans at the prospect of a camping trip, and neither cold nor hot weather slows us down.

So, take a look at this section for a few ideas, and then flip through some of the lists in Resources, beginning on page 71, and the catalogs listed beginning on page 77. As with the other sections, take what you need and leave the rest behind.

63. *Accommodations.* Where to rest your weary head is one of the first questions to settle when you decide to move beyond day-tripping. The good news is that you have a lot of choices whatever your budget, and most of those options can be rented or borrowed a few times before you buy.

Over time you'll find your own comfort zone on the continuum from Spartan to deluxe. For now, start simple and see how it works. As to where to rent or buy, take a look at the list of Resources, beginning on page 77.

64. Many state parks have *cabins for rent.* Reservation policies vary, so check with the folks at your destination as far ahead of time as possible. If you're not sure where to start, check with the Parks and Wildlife Department for the state you intend to visit. A listing of these is provided in Resources, beginning on page 83.

65. *Kampgrounds of America* (KOA) now offers their trademark Kamping Kabins, which furnish basic sleeping quarters for between $20 and $40 a night (for two to four adults or children). Not all KOAs have them; check with the Kampground nearest your destination. You'll need to provide bedding, personal items, and cooking utensils. Kabins include grills and access to all KOA amenities, such as showers, restrooms, laundry, convenience store, and sometimes swimming pools or other

recreational activities. Every Kampground has its own 800 number. Call KOA at 406-248-7444 to obtain a directory.

66. *Private cabin rentals* also are available in most well traveled tourist destinations. Depending on size, location, and amenities, you can pay anywhere from $20 to over $100 a night.

67. *Tents* are where former renters often start buying. To get up to speed quickly on what's available, take at look at the L.L. Bean, Campmor, and REI catalogs. You can usually buy a very decent tent for about $100 per person (i.e., a tent that sleeps two comfortably usually costs around $200). If you are buying the tent mail-order, check the return policy.

68. Practice setting up the tent in your yard several times (do at least one night-time practice run) before heading out. If you expect kids to sleep in the tent, a few backyard sleep-outs before the main event are a good idea.

Pros: Tents are the most inexpensive camping accommodations you can own and are highly portable. You can camp anywhere you can get permission.

Cons: A really good tent may be weatherproof, but it is still an unnerving thing to get caught out in a violent storm in a tent. A bad downpour can

"They Didn't Tell Me Nothin' 'Bout No Bulb!"

It will always be known as the Summer of the (Cursed) Houseboat. Yearning for a summer flavored get-together, Dave and his two brothers and all the respective spouses pitched in to rent a houseboat on Lake Texoma, leaving the kids with loving grandmas.

What went wrong? Pretty much everything you could imagine, short of having a bad time or sinking the (Cursed) Houseboat. Our camping barge turned out to be unsinkable, as were our spirits. We managed to laugh (later) about getting stuck in a sandbank, a sheared off prop blade, shredded gas lines in the stove, the spotlight-wielding bow-fishers that motored past our mooring one midnight, and, yes, even the external, running light bulb our roving mechanic neglected to bring, he of the now-infamous phrase, "They didn't tell me nothin' 'bout no bulb!"

Even more amazing than our eventual safe return is that we still happily remember the morning swims, evening landings on secluded rocky beached coves, fireworks on the Fourth, fishing off the stern, and chasing around the boat on rented SeaDoos one afternoon. So, I can recommend camping afloat. Just be sure to bring your toolbox!

make it difficult to get out and go to the bathroom, cook, or sleep.

69. *Recreational vehicles.* The basic choices here are motor homes, trailers, and pop-up trailers. Motor homes are motorized RVs that you can drive down the road. Trailers are hard-sided RVs you pull behind a tow vehicle, usually a pickup truck. Pop-up trailers are soft-sided RVs that fold down into a lightweight, compact size you can pull easily with a car or minivan.

    Price and comparison info is beyond the scope of this book, but be aware that there is an available supply of used RVs. Check your newspaper's want ads, and start scanning issues of *Trailer Life* and *Motor Home* magazines, or their Web sites (see Resources, beginning on page 77, for more info on these publications).

70. Our main justification for getting a modest, little, hard-sided trailer was protection from sudden weather (well, that and simplifying midnight potty runs for a recently trained little girl). But in addition to thunderstorms and cold snaps, we've also been beset by sudden swarms of flies and gusts of dust at meal-time. The trailer has enabled us to escape all airborne pestilences, while cooking and eating.

    You can achieve the same outcome with your camp stove under a tent flap with a little mosquito netting, or a net-and-nylon dining canopy over a

Happy Camper Principle IV:

The more situations you are prepared for, the more you are prepared to enjoy.

picnic table. Just remember **Happy Camper Principle IV:** *The more situations you are prepared for, the more you are prepared to enjoy.*

71. *Backpacks.* You probably already have a day-pack, and it's probably all you need. If not, check out the Army-Navy surplus store, your local sporting goods store, or a college bookstore if you live in a college town.

    Think through what you need to take and the kinds of places you'll be hiking, and you'll have a requirements list together in no time. A waterproof (or at least water-resistant) pack is a good idea, but no need to pay extra for it. Just Scotchgard your pack yourself. An outside pocket or two is handy, whether solid or mesh.

72. The most important point on packs? **Happy Camper Principle V:** *Everybody over two years of age packs her own stuff.* The goal is for any kid who's old enough to walk part or all of the hike to carry his own weight (and munchies!). My daugh-

The Luggable Child

"He ain't heavy, he's my . . . " Child, actually. I still vividly remember a Virginia Blue Ridge day-hike that a toddling Harper finished asleep on my back, her drooping body lolling in the carrier, her breath hot on my neck. She even snoozed right through a semi-perilous stream crossing.

Even now that the kids have outgrown the backpack carrier, we still occasionally find ourselves lugging a tired child over hill and dale to continue or conclude a hike. Don't tell your chiropractor this, but if you loosen the straps of your daypack, you can sling a kid onto your back in just such a way that the backpack helps cradle the precious load.

Now don't get me wrong. I do not want two-year-old, 42-pound Chandler to get used to the idea of Mom as Pack Mule. But, truth be told, there is something awfully sweet about carrying a little somebody who's old enough to say "Thanks, Mom."

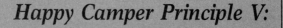

Happy Camper Principle V:

Everybody over two years of age packs her own stuff.

ter, Harper, hiked her little butt off at 18 months, and my son, Chandler, is a hiking bandit now at two. *And* he carries his own pack with diapers, wipes, spare T-shirt, and shorts. Go, boy!

73. *Camp chairs.* You'll find several models available, ranging in style from very upright chairs that prop you up at table height to more casual lounging chairs that keep you closer to the ground in a more relaxed position. Most of the places we camp have picnic tables, so we've opted for the low-to-the-ground type. They work well for grown-ups and kids; very comfy around a campfire. Get a couple to spare; they beat sitting on the ground.

74. *Rubber tubs.* We don't go anywhere without our big Rubbermaid tubs. We keep one full of firewood (it doubles as a dirty clothes hamper on the home-bound trip), and the other stows hiking boots, water shoes, lanterns, and various other bits of small gear.

75. *Camp stoves.* We have a basic Coleman stove we purchased before we got the camper (which is equipped with a nice little kitchen setup), and we

still use it when we want to cook outside, at home and on camping trips. We think getting a "dual-fuel" model is a good idea. These can run on unleaded gasoline or kerosene.

76. *Lanterns.* You can obtain these in electric or liquid fuel models. We purchased a small Coleman dual-fuel lantern, which we hang in a handy tree or on the lantern stand some campgrounds provide. We also purchased a couple of candle lanterns for the table, which cast a very nice soft glow over dinner and protect the flame from moths and wayward evening breezes.

77. *Shovel, hatchet, and knife.* Your local Army-Navy surplus store is a good place to look for these items. A folding shovel is handy for digging a fire pit or emptying a charcoal grill, and hatchets are great for chopping kindling. You can get these with leather blade guards that help keep them safe around small children.

Multifunctional Swiss Army knives are nice to have in your pack, since they can solve so many small but annoying problems.

78. *Water shoes.* You can pay a bunch of money for these. Don't. Every discount retailer carries them now for less than $10 a pair. We got ours at Walmart for less than $6, and three years later they are still wading strong.

Sandal-style water shoes are fine for pool-side, but the slipper-style shoes are much better for spending time in the water, especially where you might have unstable footing, as in a rocky beach or shoreline. Strap sandals don't offer enough support in those situations. The slipper-style also gives more protection from hot sand at the beach.

79. *Hiking boots.* As with all other camping gear, you can get basic, economically priced hiking boots, or pay for extra features. For kids, lightweight uppers and sturdy, lugged soles are the key features to look for. High ankle support and Achilles' heel cuts are helpful.

Waterproof is nice for adults who won't outgrow their boots in a year, but too expensive for kids' boots (just put trash bags over their boots and tie off with rubber bands. Little kids think this is cool!).

The Campmor and Sierra catalogs described in "Resources," page 77, have some great bargains on kids' and adults' boots.

80. If you have friends or family who camp with their kids, get in line for used boots. My daughter has worn a pair of her older cousin's boots for the last year, and my son has been wearing my daughter's work boots for hiking. These shoes tend to be durably made, so going the "pre-owned" route will save you money.

Star Spying in the Canyonlands

What do the words "West Texas" bring to mind? Well if you were driving across the plains south of Amarillo, you might think "Flat. Cow pastures. Dry and dusty. Too warm and too boring." A warning: Don't limit yourself to what you think you know, based on what you think you see.

If you happened to detour through prairie and pasture to Turkey, Texas (Bob Wills' hometown) and the nearby town of Quitaque ("kitty-kay" to the locals), you'd find verdant fields yielding to weather-etched red bluffs capped with limestone. When you catch your first glimpse of Caprock Canyons, you might think you've fallen off Texas into New Mexico.

It was on our first trip to Caprock that we discovered Harper could *hike*. Not quite two-and-a-half years old, Harper strode the two-mile Eagle Point trail with abandon, examining mysterious poops, warily eyeing cactus and yuccas, and clambering up trail-side rocks with Mom.

Quite frankly, though, the most amazing thing about West Texas is what it doesn't have: light pollution. Naked-eye stargazing is astounding, and a Celestron puts you in telescope heaven. You may find yourself torn, as we were, between fire-gazing and heaven-watching, ember-stirring and satellite-counting.

West Texas. Warm, yes . . . boring, no.

When shopping for new, if you intend to hand down a pair of boots eventually, look for gender-neutral colors. Cousin Julie's boots are purple and black, so Chandler will be wearing them this fall.

81. Got a baby? Do yourself a favor. Get yourself a stout, backpack-style, child carrier. Some people start out with front carriers for little infants, but you're probably not going to take Baby on that many hikes before five months of age or so. At that point she can hold her head well enough to sit up in the backpack carrier, which is useful a lot longer. Which is why I am not kidding about stout. You're going to be using the carrier for at least the next two years, or longer if you get suckered into kid number two, or—bless your heart—three, four . . .

82. In shopping for a backpack carrier, look for sturdy shoulder straps, a hip belt to transfer the child's weight to the hips of the person doing the carrying, and shoulder and lap belts inside the carrier to hold the kid securely.

   Several models have little packs that stow in the frame below the kid's seat. This is a nice feature, but I wouldn't bother with the "rain-hood." (Oh, right, like I'm going to lug 30 pounds of kid out into a rainstorm, or even a threat of rain!)

83. *Mountain bikes.* Most areas with good biking trails have a local outfitter who will rent bikes to you.

Some companies even specialize in bike trips where you're ferried to a starting point (no need to leave your vehicle at the trailhead), fed and watered along the route, and trundled back to your car.

If you find yourself biking more than three or four times a year, start shopping. If you are interested in riding some around town as well, check out the hybrid trail/city bikes. These have slightly less knobby tires but all the appeal of the trail bike (like grip-shifters, a dream come true for the balance-challenged among us!).

84. *Canoes* and other small, transportable watercraft also are excellent candidates for rentals (unless you frequently camp near water warm enough to enjoy three-fourths of the year, in which case you might want to buy). Most sizable lakes with tourist populations have outfitters renting canoes and personal watercraft like SeaDoos, ski boats, and sailboats.

Camper's Prayer

Creator of this earth, we give thanks to You.
It is in the cathedral of the wild
That we feel closest to You.
We feel your Spirit moving when the breeze
   touches our faces.
We see your care in the tiny details of the
   wildflowers by the trail.
We know your strength when we wonder at the
   might of the high places,
   and rest in the gentleness of the low valleys.
We hear your joy in life when soaring birds cry
   out, and song birds whistle.
We taste the freshness of your creation in the
   simple meals we make and ask You to bless.
We sing your praise when we bring our
   children up and out into the wildness of your
   making.
We feel you here with us in the place you made
   for us,
   and we are glad. We give thanks.

Amen.

6.
Sleep

My kids on a full night's sleep are different kids than when sleep-deprived. In fact, I have a theory that most juvenile delinquents getting into trouble today are just feeling the effects of years of sleep deprivation. Maybe if we just put them all to bed for 10 hours a day for a few years . . . oh well. Back to the point at hand. **Happy Camper Principle VI:** *Sleep is an important prerequisite to having fun on camping trips. Make sure the kids and the adults get plenty.*

85. Schedule is important for my kids' sleep habits. Fact is, they *have* sleep habits, which I have carefully reinforced over the years with rituals and schedules. I maintain those rituals and schedules as nearly as possible on camping trips, for both naps and bedtime.

Happy Camper Principle VI:

Sleep is an important prerequisite to having fun on camping trips. Make sure the kids and the adults get plenty.

86. Nap follows hard on the heels of lunch, and we usually don't have a problem with it, since the kids are tuckered out from the morning's activities, and their bellies are full. So they get that nice logy feeling, and Mom tucks them in . . . and then it's party-time! Well, for the adults anyway.

87. At night we have what we call the Big Slide to bedtime: the progression flows from dinner, to bath, into jammies, with bedtime stories, prayers, hugs and kisses, and then lights out. Of these, the bath is the most tempting to skip, but we always try to get one in, since it seems to really cue my kids' subconscious that it's bedtime.

    Of course, sometimes we derail our own best laid plans by lingering overlong 'round the campfire, reading bedtime stories . . . but hey, that's what camping is for, right?

88. Build enthusiasm ahead of time for whatever the sleeping arrangements are going to be, to help create a fun adventure. Our camper has a full-size foldout bed for the grown-ups, a slide-out twin-size bed, and a foldout shelf of a twin bed above the full-size bed.

    To help Harper (three years old at the time) get into the foldout bed (mentally and physically), we let her pick out a kid sleeping bag with her favorite Disney character on it and talked about it for weeks before our first trip. She was so excited she

Amazing Grace at Cedar Lake

A recent camping trip deliberately close to home ended up taking me many miles and years away.

Camped at Cleburne State Park on tiny Cedar Lake, we were enjoying an evening bonfire, debating whether to mosey over to the natural amphitheater to hear Cowboy Poetry Night.

Suddenly a humming intake of air broke the evening's calm with a boisterous blow. Our neighbors across the road included a bagpiper, and he'd begun an evening serenade.

We drew closer in the dark, each with a child on hip, listening with shivers and tingles to the stirring music, skillfully played. We spoke of feeling transported to a distant isle, sentimental and green at dusk.

Then the piper started a new song with a strong breath, and things got personal. It was "Amazing Grace," my grandmother's favorite hymn. I hadn't heard it since her funeral less than a year ago. I couldn't stop the tears that came, but I sang the song to Chandler, who carries her maiden name: Wilma Lura Chandler. I told him that was Grannybopper's favorite song.

As the song faded into the night, we returned to the fire and stirred the embers alight. That was poetry enough.

almost flew up into the bed. Dave built a bed rail to help her stay in, and stay she does. She loves her little aerie.

89. When we first started using the trailer, Chandler was 14 months old and still needed confinement to get to sleep. We put his portable crib on the slide-out twin bed and put him in it. However, by 18 months we had him in a twin bed at home with a bed rail. So now we bring the bed rail with us and slide the bed out partway, and he has a cozy little nest of his own. He stays in it for the most part. We just try to wear him out during the day so he's too pooped to stir up much trouble at night.

90. One little trick that helps us at nap- and night-time is to keep things the adults might need while the kids are sleeping *outside* the trailer, tent, or cabin, including jackets, firewood, cooler of ice and/or drinks, books, lanterns, camping chairs. That way we can let sleeping babies lie, which leads to all sorts of interesting evenings. But that's another book . . .

7.
Conclusion

Sounds easy enough, doesn't it? Sure it does. Go on, now that you've got some kindling together, put a big log on the fire!

Don't forget to send me a postcard to tell me who went where, how much fun you had, and what you learned. I can't wait to hear.

8.

Resources: Additional Information You Might Find Useful

The Lists: Planning, Packing, and Preparing

As mentioned in Tip #2, my primary list has three columns: Week Before, Day Before, and Day of Trip. I keep it in a three-column format so I can fold it to the appropriate view. It looks like this. (See below for detail on list contents.)

Week Before	Day Before	Day Of Trip
❏ Xxxxxxxxxxxxx	❏ Xxxxxxxxxxxxx	❏ Xxxxxxxxxxxxx
❏ Xxxxxxxxxxxxx	❏ Xxxxxxxxxxxxx	❏ Xxxxxxxxxxxxx
❏ Xxxxxxxxxxxxxxxx	❏ Xxxxxxxxxxxxxxxx	❏ Xxxxxxxxxxxxxxxx
❏ Xxxxxxxxxxxx	❏ Xxxxxxxxxxxx	❏ Xxxxxxxxxxxx
❏ Xxxxxxxxxxxxx	❏ Xxxxxxxxxxxxx	❏ Xxxxxxxxxxxxx
❏ Xxxxxxxxxxxxx		❏ Xxxxxxxxxxxxx
❏ Xxxxxxxxxxxx	❏ Xxxxxxxxxxxxxxxxxx	❏ Xxxxxxxxxxxx
❏ Xxxxxxxxxxxxxxxxxxx	❏ Xxxxxxxxxxxxx	❏ Xxxxxxxxxxxxxxxxxxx
❏ Xxxxxxxxxxxx	❏ Xxxxxxxxxxxxx	❏ Xxxxxxxxxxxx
❏ Xxxxxxxxxxxxx	❏ Xxxxxxxxxxxxx	❏ Xxxxxxxxxxxxx
❏ Xxxxxxxxxxxxxxxxx	❏ Xxxxxxxxxxxxxxxx	❏ Xxxxxxxxxxxxx
❏ Xxxxxxxxxxxxx	❏ Xxxxxxxxxxxxxxxx	❏ _____
❏ Xxxxxxxxxxxx	❏ Xxxxxxxxxxxxx	❏ _____
❏ Xxxxxxxxxxxx	❏ Xxxxxxxxxxxxx	❏ _____
❏ Xxxxxxxxxxxxx	❏ Xxxxxxxxxxxxx	❏ _____
❏ Xxxxxxxxxxxxx	❏ Xxxxxxxxxxxxxxxx	❏ _____
❏ Xxxxxxxxxxxxxxxxx		

Week Before

Week Before includes "permanent" and "consumable" stocks. *Consumables* include non-refrigerated and refrigerated food, listed separately to aid in packing.

Permanent stocks are those items we usually keep packed to go, but sometimes "borrow" out of camp storage or bring in for a thorough cleaning. Before the trip, I make sure these items are in the camper, and replace them if necessary.

- ❏ kid cups
- ❏ towels
- ❏ camping chairs
- ❏ Lexan utensils
- ❏ camera
- ❏ binoculars
- ❏ weather radio
- ❏ small cutting board
- ❏ backpack carrier

Consumable stocks are the things we always use up eventually. Every trip I check to see what we've used up on the last trip and need to replenish. Non-food items include:

- ❏ wipes, dipes
- ❏ toilet paper
- ❏ RV toilet chemicals
- ❏ trash bags (big, small)
- ❏ firewood
- ❏ fire starters
- ❏ charcoal
- ❏ foil
- ❏ batteries (AA, D)
- ❏ Zip-locs
- ❏ paper towels, plates
- ❏ camera film

We list food under *Consumables* as well. This list includes a lot of optional items as idea triggers. What we take on each trip varies and may include:

Non-refrigerated
- ☐ bread
- ☐ salt/pepper
- ☐ olive oil
- ☐ pasta
- ☐ rice-in-bags
- ☐ canned potatoes
- ☐ canned beans
- ☐ cereal
- ☐ juice boxes
- ☐ evaporated or dry milk
- ☐ crackers, chips
- ☐ chocolate bars
- ☐ graham crackers
- ☐ marshmallows
- ☐ Nutri-grain bars
- ☐ granola bars

Refrigerated
- ☐ coffee
- ☐ club soda
- ☐ fruit, veggies
- ☐ cheese
- ☐ eggs
- ☐ butter
- ☐ mayo, mustard
- ☐ pesto
- ☐ ice cream (quarts)
- ☐ roasted chicken
- ☐ steaks, hamburger
- ☐ lunch meat, hot dogs
- ☐ milk
- ☐ tortillas
- ☐ sandwich pickles, relish

Day Before

The Day Before list is primarily organized to get everything packed and as much loaded and done as possible the day before departure.

Check tire pressure
- ❏ truck
- ❏ trailer

Fill truck with premium gas

Get cash

Pack duffels
- ❏ clothes
- ❏ underwear, socks
- ❏ jammies
- ❏ hiking boots
- ❏ water sandals
- ❏ camper shoes
- ❏ jackets
- ❏ long underwear

Pack kit bags
- ❏ shampoo
- ❏ contact stuff
- ❏ sunscreen
- ❏ kid medicine
- ❏ grown-up medicine
- ❏ glasses
- ❏ hair bands, clips
- ❏ deodorant

Pack road-trip backpacks
- ❏ dipes, wipes
- ❏ changing pad
- ❏ snacks
- ❏ books
- ❏ coloring books, colors
- ❏ brush, hair bands

Day of Trip

The Day of Trip list helps you get out the door and on the road without forgetting the things you really can't or don't want to do till the last minute. For us, that includes:

Load trailer
- ☐ duffels
- ☐ sleeping bags, sheet
- ☐ pillows
- ☐ cold food in fridge
- ☐ ice, drinks in cooler or freezer
- ☐ doormat
- ☐ Chandler's bed rail

Take out trash

Load truck
- ☐ backpacks
- ☐ book box
- ☐ road snacks
- ☐ road cups/drinks
- ☐ Coleman stove
- ☐ Coleman lantern
- ☐ compressor, gauges
- ☐ tool kit
- ☐ firewood box
- ☐ bikes, helmets
- ☐ maps, other directions

Magazines, Catalogs, and Web Sites

Family Camping. This newish magazine by Rodale Press has a nice mix of stories on family oriented camping gear, places to stay, things to do, ways to save money. Must have some parents on the staff! The downside is it's only published twice a year and is not available by subscription. If they get enough new readers, maybe they'll start bringing it out more often and offering subscriptions. Call 800-480-1110 for information about retailers that carry it.

Backpacker. Aimed at "wilderness travelers." Not family-specific, but lots of useful knowledge for all campers. Published nine times a year by Rodale Press. For subscription information call 800-666-3434.

Trailer Life and *Motor Home.* Aimed at retired adults, these magazines are, nonetheless, good sources of information about pull-behind trailers, towing vehicles and motor homes, as well as after-market items (items you might buy to repair or enhance your trailer or motor home) RVers of any age might need. You can find some destination ideas as well. For subscription information on *Trailer Life* or *Motor Home,* call 800-825-6861. *Trailer Life* also has a Web page; see www.trailerlife.com.

StarDate is the name of the radio show and magazine put out by the McDonald Observatory Public Information Office, associated with the University of Texas at Austin. Each magazine includes star charts for the two months covered by the bimonthly issue, in addition to articles of interest to amateur astronomers and more casual stargazers. You can also find StarDate on the Web at http://stardate.utexas.edu. For more information check the Web site, where there's lots to do and look at, including a form to order a sample issue of the magazine, or call 800-STARDATE.

REI. We've rented equipment several times from REI, a co-op retailer specializing in outdoor gear and clothing. Call 800-426-4840 for the location nearest you, or to obtain a catalog.

Get a membership the first year you start camping. You may be getting quite a bit of stuff, and the membership gets you a rebate of 10 percent on everything you buy (except sale items). Do watch for the sales. We got a good deal on a couple of nice mountain bikes one Christmas.

L.L. Bean. Has several outdoor, sporting specialty, mail-order catalogs of clothing (for all ranges of weather), equipment (everything from mountain bikes to canoes), and gear (for everybody from the yuppies to the real mountaineers), including L.L. Bean Kids, Camping, season-specific Sports, Women's, etc.

Periodically throughout the year, each catalog discounts slow-moving or overstocked merchandise, so keep a sharp eye out. (We have compared prices between L.L. Bean, Sierra Trading Post, Campmor and local discount retailers on things we want to buy. When L.L. Bean discounts an item, they are competitive with the others. However, day-in, day-out prices are higher.)

They are known for excellent customer service and product quality, and we've always had good dealings with them.

You probably already receive one or more of their catalogs. If not, or if you don't get one that has what you want, call 800-221-4221, or visit them on the Web at www.llbean.com.

Campmor. Another discount mail-order catalog specializing in sporting gear, clothing, and equipment. Huge selection with pretty good prices, including a range of tent styles and sizes for those of you going light on infrastructure.
They carry kids' stuff, and many of the same brand names as L.L. Bean, usually with lower prices (sometimes a lot lower). Call 800-CAMPMOR (800-226-7667) for a catalog, or visit their Web site at www.campmor.com.

Sierra Trading Post. Discount mail-order catalog of sporting gear, clothing, and equipment. Sierra offers overstocks and closeouts they've picked up from name-brand marketers like Merrell, Hind, New Balance, and others; some seconds with minor blemishes. Limited selection, but discounts are significant, from 35-70 percent. Sierra has two outlet stores, one in Reno and one in Cheyenne. The rest of us can get their catalog by calling 800-713-4534.

After the Stork. Mail-order catalog (one company store at headquarters in Albuquerque) specializing in cotton kids' clothing. The Stork offers a good value on kids' long underwear basics in plain or thermal cotton knit, in a rainbow of colors and sizes. Good selection of sturdy shoes and boots, too. Call 800-441-4775 for a catalog.
The Stork also has begun holding Warehouse Sales around the country, where they offer discontinued and overstock items in a variety of sizes and styles. You can get some *outrageous* bargains. I once got a $15.00 long-sleeve, full-leg thermal romper for my son for $3.00.
Call the Warehouse Sale Hotline at 800-826-0619 for more

information. Their email address is storkmail@ afterthestork.com. See their Web page at www.afterthe stork.com.

Texas Parks and Wildlife. The Web site for this state agency is outstanding. Take a look at http://www. tpwd.state.tx.us/tpwd.htm. You'll find descriptions of all state parks, including available attractions, amenities, and lodging options. You can also reach the TP&W agency at its general information line number: 800-792-1112. (Note: Names and addresses of other state agencies of this type can be found in Resources, beginning on page 83.)

World Wide Wilderness Directory. This on-line public access forum, located at www.wbm.ca/wilderness, provides information regarding all kinds of outdoor services. You can find information about many outdoor adventure opportunities, including wilderness eco-tourism treks, whitewater rafting, canoeing, camping, family and corporate packages, hunting and fishing outfitters, even luxurious five-star resorts. This Web service gives adventure outfitters everywhere in the world the capability to list their offerings.

The directory service is available to adventure camps, outfitters, camp owners or their agents (including group associations), and regional, provincial/state, and federal tourism authorities.

US National Park Service. Aka Parknet: The National Park Service Place on the Net is located at www.nps.gov. This Web site offers a lot more than camping information. The opening screen offers hotlinks not only to information about every park in the system, but also special sections on Links to the Past: America's Histories and Cultures; Park Smart: Education and Interpretation; Info Zone: Service-wide Information; and Nature Net: Nature Resources in the Parks.

Parknet also links to the National Park Foundation's on-line **Park Store,** connecting you to an increasingly wide array of Park-related products and services that you can order or purchase over the Internet, or by phone or fax. The Park Store is designed as a gateway to the best National Park publications, maps, videos, tours, collectibles, and a wealth of other products to help you plan, enjoy, and remember your National Park adventures.

Now available: *The Complete Guide to America's Parks,* a traveler's guide to all 369 units in America's National Park System, and *Trails Illustrated Maps,* high quality, richly detailed maps of the National Parks for a wide range of uses, from hiking to sightseeing.

US Fish and Wildlife also has a page, more oriented toward fish and game management than camping and hiking, but, if you are interested, take a look at www.fws.gov.

United States Geological Survey. Established by the US Department of the Interior, the USGS is the nation's largest earth science research and information agency. You can visit their page at www.usgs.gov. The USGS provides "geologic, topographic, and hydrologic information in the form of maps, databases, descriptions, and analyses of the water, energy, and mineral resources, land surface, underlying geologic structure, natural hazards, and dynamic processes of the earth."

If you've never seen a USGS topo map, try ordering one for your area, or a place you know and love. Look in your phone book's Yellow Pages, or call 800-HELP-MAP, or write: USGS Information Services, Box 25286, Denver Federal Center, Denver, CO 80225.

Parks Canada. This is the management organization for the national parks system in Canada. You can reach them by phone at (819) 997-0055. Their TDD number is (819)994-4957, and their email address is parks_webmaster@pch.gc.ca. You can write to the national office at: Parks Canada National Office, 25 Eddy Street, Hull, Quebec, Canada, K1A 0M5.

Parks Canada's Web site is simply phenomenal; point your browser at http://parkscanada.pch.gc.ca/. This site offers a wealth of information in English and French (you can switch languages on many of the pages). At the main screen, you can select *Visit Us*; this displays listings on Cultural Heritage, Natural Heritage, and Cooperative Heritage Initiatives. Click on *National Heritage* to select National Parks; on this page, you can choose whether you want to see an alphabetical list of all the parks, or an alphabetical list of parks by province. Once at this list, you can select any park and visit its dedicated page, which will display options for just about anything you want to know, including how to reach the park by mail or phone, how to travel to it, what its featured attractions are, description of its historical background, among other options.

Great Outdoor Recreation Pages. This on-line-only resource is not to be missed; see www.gorp.com. According to the publishers, Diane and Bill Greer, GORP is a Web site packed with valuable information of interest to outdoor recreationists and active travelers. You'll find information on traveling the world.

Attractions lists national parks, forests, wildernesses, wildlife refuges, historic sites, and more, describing where to go and what to do on lands throughout the United States.

Activities helps the outdoor enthusiast in pursuit of just about anything: hiking, biking, fishing, paddling, skiing, birding.

Locations lets you throw a dart at the world map and learn about whatever distant corner the point hits. Books, gear, tours, recipes, art . . . if it has an outdoor and active travel theme, it's fair game for GORP.

Alphabetical List of U.S. Parks and Wildlife Departments and Canadian National Parks

For more information on places to go and things to do, you may want to contact the department of parks and wildlife for the state or province you are interested in visiting.

Alabama Department of Game and Fish
64 N. Union St.
Montgomery, AL 36130
(205) 261-3486

Alaska Department of Fish and Game
P.O. Box 3-2000
Juneau, AK 99802
(907) 465-4100

Arizona Game and Fish Department
Arizona State Parks
2222 W. Greenway Road
Phoenix, AZ 85023
(602) 942-3000

Arkansas Game and Fish Commission
2 Natural Resources Drive
Little Rock, AR 72205
(501) 223-6300

California Department of Fish and Game
1416 Ninth Street
Sacramento, CA 95814
(916) 445-3531

California Department of Parks and Recreation
1416 Ninth Street
Sacramento, CA 95814
(916) 653-6995

Colorado Department of Natural Resources
1313 Sherman Street, Room #718
Denver, CO 80203
(303) 866-3311

Connecticut Department of Environmental Protection
165 Capitol Avenue
Hartford, CT 06106
(203) 566-5599

Delaware Division of Fish and Wildlife
P.O. Box 1401
Dover, DE 19903
(302) 736-4431

Delaware Division of Parks and Recreation
89 Kings Highway
P.O. Box 1401
Dover, DE 19903
(302) 739-4413

Florida Game and Freshwater Fish Commission
620 S. Meridan Street
Tallahassee, FL 32399-1500
(904) 488-1960

Florida Marine Fisheries Commission
2540 Executive Center, Circle West
Tallahassee, FL 32301
(904) 447-0554

Georgia Department of Natural Resources
205 Butler Street
Atlanta, GA 30334
(404) 656-3510

Hawaii Department of Land and Natural Resources
1151 Punchbowl Street
Honolulu, HI 96813
(808) 548-4000

Idaho Fish and Game Department
Idaho Department of Parks and Recreation
600 South Walnut Street
P.O. Box 25
Boise, ID 83707
(208) 334-3700

Illinois Department of Conservation
524 S. Second Street
Springfield, IL 62701
(217) 782-6302

Indiana Department of Natural Resources
402 W. Washington Street
Indianaplis, IN 46204
(317) 232-4020

Iowa Department of Natural Resources
Wallace State Office Building
E. Ninth and Grand Ave.
Des Moines, IA 50319
(515) 281-5145

Kansas Department of Wildlife & Parks
RR 2, Box 54A
Pratt, KS 67124
(316) 672-5911

Kentucky Department of Fish and Wildlife
1 Game Farm Road
Frankfort, KY 40601
(502) 564-3400

Kentucky Department of Parks
Capital Plaza Tower, 500 Mero St., Suite 1100
Frankfort, KY 40601-1974
(800) 255-PARK

Louisiana Department of Wildlife and Fisheries
P.O. Box 98000
Baton Rouge, LA 70898
(504) 765-2800

Maine Department of Inland Fisheries and Wildlife
284 State Street Station #41
Augusta, ME 04333
(207) 289-2766

Maryland Department of Natural Resources
Tawes State Office Building
580 Taylor Avenue
Annapolis, MD 21401
(301) 974-3990

**Massachusetts Department of Fisheries,
Wildlife and Environmental Law Enforcement**
100 Cambridge Street
Boston, MA 02202
(617) 727-1614

Michigan Department of Natural Resources
P.O. Box 30028
Lansing, MI 48909
(517) 373-1220

Minnesota Department of Natural Resources
Division of Fish and Wildlife
500 Lafayette Road
St. Paul, MN 55155
(612) 296-6157

Mississippi Department of Wildlife Conservation
P.O. Box 451
Jackson, MS 39205
(601) 362-9219

Missouri Department of Conservation
P.O. Box 180
Jefferson City, MO 65102
(314) 751-4115

Montana Department of Fish and Wildlife
1420 E. Sixth
Helena, MT 59620
(406) 444-2535

Nebraska Game and Parks Commission
2200 N. 33rd Street
P.O. Box 30370
Lincoln, NE 68503
(402) 464-0641

Nevada Department of Wildlife
P.O. Box 10678
Reno, NV 89520
(702) 789-0500

New Hampshire Fish and Game Department
2 Hazen Drive
Concord, NH 03301
(603) 271-3421

New Jersey Division of Fish, Game, and Wildlife
401 E. State Street CN402
Trenton, NJ 08625
(609) 292-2695

New Mexico Game and Fish Department
Villagra Building
Santa Fe, NM 87503
(505) 827-7899

New York Deparment of Fish and Wildlife
50 Wolf Road
Albany, NY 12233
(518) 457-5690

North Carolina Wildlife Resources Commission
Archdal Building
512 N. Salisbury Street
Raleigh, NC 27611
(919) 733-3391

North Dakota State Game and Fish Department
100 N. Bismark Expressway
Bismark, ND 58501
(701) 221-6300

Ohio Department of Natural Resources
Division of Wildlife
Fountain Square
Columbus, OH 43224
(614) 265-6565

Oklahoma Department of Wildlife Conservation
P.O. Box 53465
1801 N. Lincoln
Oklahoma City, OK 73152
(405) 521-3851

Oregon Department of Fish and Wildlife
P.O. Box 59
Portland, OR 97207
(502) 299-5551

Pennsylvania Game Commission
2001 Elmerton Avenue
Harrisburg, PA 17110
(717) 787-4250

Rhode Island Department of Environmental Management
22 Hayes Street
Providence, RI 02908
(401) 277-2774

South Carolina Department of Natural Resources
P.O. Box 167
Columbia, SC 29202
(803) 734-3888

South Dakota Game, Fish, and Parks
445 E. Capitol
Pierre, SD 57501
(605) 773-3888

Tennessee Wildlife Resources Agency
Ellington Agricultural Center
P.O. Box 40747
Nashville, TN 37204
(615) 781-6500

Texas Parks and Wildlife
4200 Smith School Road
Austin, TX 78744
(512) 389-4800

Utah State Department of Natural Resources
1596 W. North Temple
Salt Lake City, UT 84116
(801) 538-4700

Vermont Fish and Wildlife Department
103 S. Main Street
Waterbury Complex
Waterbury, VT 05676
(802) 244-7331

Virginia Department of Game and Inland Fisheries
4010 W. Broad Street
P.O. Box 11104
Richmond, VA 23230
(804) 367-1000

Washington Department of Fish and Wildlife
600 Capitol Way N.
Olympia, WA 98501-1091
(206) 753-5700

Washington State Parks and Recreation Commission
P.O. Box 42650
Olympia, WA 98504-2650
(800) 233-0321

West Virginia Department of Natural Resources
1900 Kanawha Boulevard E.
Charleston, WV 25305
(304) 348-2754

Wisconsin Department of Natural Resources
P.O. Box 7921
Madison, WI 53707
(608) 266-2621

Wyoming Game and Fish Department
5400 Bishop Boulevard
Cheyenne, WY 82006
(307) 777-4600

Canadian National Park Service Centers and Parks

Calgary Service Centre
Room 552
220-4th Avenue S.E.
Calgary, Alberta
Canada T2G 4X3
Telephone: (403) 292-4401 or 1-800-748-7275
Fax: (403) 292-6004
Email (Manitoba, Saskatchewan, Alberta, Northwest
Territories): NatlParks-AB@pch.gc.ca
Email (British Columbia): py_infocentre@pch.gc.ca

Alberta national parks include:

Banff National Park. UNESCO World Heritage Site
and Canada's first National Park (1885).

Elk Island National Park. Alberta plains oasis for rare
and endangered species.

Jasper National Park. UNESCO World Heritage Site
and glacial jewel of the Rockies.

Waterton Lakes National Park. International Peace
Park near the Rocky rises from grasslands.

Wood Buffalo National Park. UNESCO World
Heritage Site larger than Switzerland.

British Columbia national parks include:

Glacier National Park. British Columbia's lush interior rainforest and permanent glaciers.

Gwaii Haanas National Park Reserve. Haïda culture and coastal rainforest on Queen Charlotte Islands.

Kootenay National Park. UNESCO World Heritage Site featuring the famous Radium Hot Springs.

Mount Revelstoke National Park. Rainforest of 1,000-year-old cedars and spectacular mountains.

Pacific Rim National Park Reserve. Pacific Coast Mountains make up this marine and forest environment.

Yoho National Park. UNESCO World Heritage Site in Rockies.

Manitoba national parks include:

Riding Mountain National Park. Protected "island" area in the Manitoba Escarpment.

Wapusk National Park. One of the largest polar bear denning areas in the world.

Northwest Territories national parks include:

Aulavik National Park. Over 12,000 square kilometers of arctic wilderness on Banks Island.

Auyuittuq National Park Reserve. Baffin Island landscapes containing northern extremity of Canadian Shield.

Ellesmere Island National Park Reserve. Most remote, fragile, rugged and northerly lands in North America.

Tuktut Nogait National Park. Calving ground for the Bluenose caribou herd.

Nahanni National Park Reserve. Northwest Territories' UNESCO World Heritage Site.

Wood Buffalo National Park. UNESCO World Heritage Site larger than Switzerland.

Saskatchewan national parks include:

Grasslands National Park. Saskatchewan's rare prairie grasses, dinosaur fossils, and badlands.

Prince Albert National Park. Protects slice of northern coniferous forest and widlife.

Halifax Service Center
Historic Properties
1869 Upper Water Street
Halifax, Nova Scotia
Canada B3J 1S9
Telephone: (902) 426-3436 or 1-800-213-7275
Fax: (902) 426-6881
Email: atlantic_parksinfo@pch.gc.ca

Nova Scotia national parks include:

Cape Breton Highlands National Park. Home to Cabot Trail, a land blessed with spectacular cliffs.

Kejimkujik National Park. Nova Scotia's inland of historic canoe routes and portages.

Quebec Service Center
3 Passage du Chien d'Or
P.O. Box 6060,
Haute-Ville
Quebec City, Quebec
Canada G1R 4V7
Telephone: (418) 648-4177 or 1-800-463-6769
Fax: (418) 649-6140
TDD: (418) 648-5099
Email: webinfo@sunqbc.
risq.net

Quebec national parks include:

Forillon National Park. The "Jewel of the Gaspé" where land meets sea.

La Mauricie National Park. Lakes winding through forested hills for canoe and portage activities.

Mingan Archipelago National Park Reserve. A string of islands carved out by wind and sea.

Ontario Service Center
111 Water Street East
Cornwall, Ontario
Canada K6H 6S3
Telephone: 1-800-839-8221
Fax: (613) 938-5729

Ontario national parks include:

Bruce Peninsula National Park. Landscapes including the northern end of Niagara Escarpment.

Georgian Bay Islands National Park. Captivating islands representing Lake Huron's landscape.

Point Pelee National Park. Most southerly point on Canadian mainland.

Pukaskwa National Park. Canadian Shield's ancient landscape on Superior's North Shore.

St. Lawrence Islands National Park. Canada's smallest national park located in Ontario.

Yukon Service Centre
Suite 205 - 300
Main Street
Whitehorse, Yukon
Canada Y1A 2B5
Telephone:1-800-661-0486
Fax: (867) 393-6701
Email: whitehorse_info@
    pch.gc.ca

Yukon national parks include:

Ivvavik National Park. Calving ground for the
Porcupine caribou herd.

Kluane National Park Reserve. Yukon's UNESCO
World Heritage Site contains Canada's highest peak.

Vuntut National Park. Northern Yukon's unique non-
glaciated landscape.

*Additional national parks are located in New Brunswick,
Newfoundland, Labrador, and Prince Edward Island. Check
the Web pages for these parks, or contact the national office.*

New Brunswick national parks include:

Fundy National Park. Atlantic's sanctuary with
world's highest tides.

Kouchibouguac National Park. Intricate Acadian
blend of coastal and inland habitats.

Newfoundland and Labrador national parks include:

Gros Morne National Park. UNESCO World Heritage Site amid Newfoundland's wild natural beauty.

Terra Nova National Park. Remnants of the Eastern Newfoundland Ancient Appalachian Mountains.

Prince Edward Island is the location of the:

Prince Edward Island National Park. A protected area with spectacular coast.

Camping Notes

_____

_____

_____

_____

_____

_____

_____

_____

_____

_____

_____

_____

_____

_____

_____

_____

_____

_____

_____

_____

_____

Camping Notes

_____

_____

_____

_____

_____

_____

_____

_____

_____

_____

_____

_____

_____

_____

_____

_____

_____

_____

_____

_____

_____

_____

_____

Camping Notes

_____

_____

_____

_____

_____

_____

_____

_____

_____

_____

_____

_____

_____

_____

_____

_____

_____

_____

_____

_____

_____

Camping Notes

_____

_____

_____

_____

_____

_____

_____

_____

_____

_____

_____

_____

_____

_____

_____

_____

_____

_____

_____

_____

Camping Notes

_____

_____

_____

_____

_____

_____

_____

_____

_____

_____

_____

_____

_____

_____

_____

_____

_____

_____

_____

_____

_____

_____

_____

_____

About the Author

Tammerie Spires and her family live in Richardson, Texas, where she is a parent, camper, gardener, and freelance writer.

She has worked in various editing positions for *Third Coast,* the city magazine for Austin, Texas, and for three computer journals. More recently she was a staff writer for Price Waterhouse LLP, preparing books and multimedia for inhouse and trade use.

Tammerie is an active member of Peace Mennonite Church in Dallas, Texas.